King Vulture

by Julie Murray

Abdo Kids
ROYAL ANIMALS

Abdo Kids Jumbo is an Imprint of Abdo Kids
abdobooks.com

abdobooks.com

Published by Abdo Kids, a division of ABDO, P.O. Box 398166, Minneapolis, Minnesota 55439.

Abdo Kids Jumbo™ is a trademark and logo of Abdo Kids.

Printed in the United States of America, North Mankato, Minnesota.

102024

012025

THIS BOOK CONTAINS RECYCLED MATERIALS

Photo Credits: Alamy, Getty Images, Shutterstock, ©Wagner Souza e Silva p21 / CC BY-SA 4.0

Production Contributors: Teddy Borth, Jennie Forsberg, Grace Hansen
Design Contributors: Candice Keimig, Pakou Moua

Library of Congress Control Number: 2024936618

Publisher's Cataloging-in-Publication Data

Names: Murray, Julie, author.

Title: King vulture / by Julie Murray

Description: Minneapolis, Minnesota : Abdo Kids, 2025 | Series: Royal animals | Includes online resources and index.

Identifiers: ISBN 9798384902997 (lib. bdg.) | ISBN 9798384903697 (ebook) | ISBN 9798384904045 (Read-to-me ebook)

Subjects: LCSH: King vulture--Juvenile literature. | Vultures--Juvenile literature. | Birds--Juvenile literature. | Rain forest animals--Juvenile literature. | Animal kingdom--Juvenile literature.

Classification: DDC 598.92--dc23

Table of Contents

The King Vulture

The king vulture is a large bird that lives in southern Mexico, Central America, and South America. It is mainly found in tropical lowland forests.

Mexico
Central America
King vulture range
South America
N
W
E
S

Its royal name comes from a **Mayan** legend. In the legend, a king vulture is a messenger between gods and humans.

Body

The king vulture is big! It can grow 2.5 feet (0.8 m) long from head to tail. It can weigh up to 10 pounds (4.5 kg).

The king vulture is more colorful than other vultures. It is white with a grayish black tail and wing tips. Its head and neck area are bald and bright in color.

The vulture's head and neck are a mix of orange, yellow, blue, red, and purple. An orange **caruncle** stands out on its beak.

Flying High

The king vulture is an excellent flyer. It has a **wingspan** of up to 7 feet (2.1 m)! It can **soar** high above the treetops for hours without flapping its wings.

Food

The king vulture is a **scavenger** that eats **carrion**. All other birds move away from the feeding site when a king vulture arrives.

The king vulture has a thick, strong beak. The beak is good for tearing into meat. The vulture also has long, sharp claws that easily hold onto food.

Baby King Vultures

Female king vultures lay a single egg. Both parents **incubate** the egg. The egg hatches in about 55 days. The chick needs its parents for the first four months of life.

More Facts

- The king vulture has a lifespan of 30 to 40 years.
- Excluding condors, king vultures are the largest of the New World vultures.
- The king vulture covers its legs in its poop. This helps the vulture to keep cool on hot days. It also keeps insects away.

Glossary

carrion – dead and rotting flesh.

caruncle – the fleshy wattle on a king vulture's beak.

incubate – to keep warm until time to hatch.

Maya – a group of people who lived in an ancient Indian civilization in Mexico and Central America.

scavenger – an animal that finds and eats dead animals.

soar – to fly or glide in a swift and easy way.

wingspan – the distance from the tip of one wing of a bird to the tip of the other.

Index